Journey with the Minor Prophets
A 12-week Bible Study

By Mary Cooney

ACKNOWLEDGEMENTS
In addition to my gratitude to God for allowing me to work on this study, I want to acknowledge and thank Vanessa Downs and Yvonne Aaseth for their invaluable help with reviewing and editing!
And thanks to Sarah Merkel who provided the beautiful cover photo!

Contents

Page

Lesson 1: Introduction	5
Lesson 2: Hosea	11
Lesson 3: Joel	17
Lesson 4: Amos	23
Lesson 5: Obadiah, Nahum, Jonah	29
Lesson 6: Micah	35
Lesson 7: Zephaniah	41
Lesson 8: Habakkuk	45
Lesson 9: Haggai	51
Lesson 10: Zechariah Part 1	55
Lesson 11: Zechariah Part 2	63
Lesson 12: Malachi	69
Charts and Timelines	75

Introduction to the Minor Prophets

Lesson 1

Welcome to our study of the Minor Prophets! What an adventure we have in store for us. Most people can't find the minor prophets in their Bibles much less who they were and what they can mean to us. Spanning centuries, they were real people with faults and foibles and sometimes their messages were less clear to them than they are to us. Most came at pivotal points in history to warn, exhort and encourage. All of them believed utterly that God is and always will be who He says He is. Look for these things as we journey. What can they teach us about living our lives today?

These studies are not intended to give you the last word on the subject nor provide you with all the answers. The goal is to engage your heart with the living Word. As we spend time alone with God asking ourselves difficult questions, we yield our hearts to the work the Holy Spirit wants to accomplish in each of us. Yet it is the corporate time in class together as we bounce ideas off one another and discover new ways of seeing an old truth that we feel the amazement of loving and being loved for who we are, naked before God.

As you well know, today we have hundreds of commentaries available to us. God has given us His inspired Word and the Holy Spirit. Let's first do our own study, ask our own questions and come to our own conclusions. *Then* if time allows, we can consult a reliable, conservative commentary.

In the Hebrew Bible, this section is called the Book of the Twelve, as it was originally a scroll that contained these twelve books. In our English Bibles, we call them the Minor Prophets, not because what they had to say was of minor importance, but simply because they are shorter than the other, Major prophets of Isaiah, Jeremiah, Ezekiel and Daniel. As you read through the books you will see the near and far prophecies all mixed together. At one moment, the prophet will be speaking; at the next ,God speaks. Remember, we can't expect "linear thinking" (western style) in a Hebrew context! (Think rather of a wheel with spokes going out from the center.)

Each lesson is divided into three sections:

Historical Background will help you put the prophet into the context in which he lived.

Under ***Scriptural Context,*** we will study the text, always looking for what it is God wants each of us to take away from the message. I will always ask you to notice what we can learn about God. I highlight these passages in yellow in my Bible. That makes them easy for me to find later.

The last section, **Personal Holiness,** will focus on what it all means to me. This study requires a lot of intellectual exercise as you learn the history of Israel and begin to see God's big picture of time and eternity.

But let's not lose sight of today. Obviously, the main point of Bible Study is to get to know God better and learn to "walk in a manner worthy of His calling." So keep that in mind as you study. Don't leave these blank. Please allow the Holy Spirit opportunity to seep truth into your life. It may not be appropriate to share in larger groups, but hopefully in your smaller groups you can keep one another accountable.

If you have taken an Old Testament survey class, you will find the going much easier. If not, don't worry. I will bring you up to speed, but you will just have to expect to work a little harder! So make your personal commitment and pace yourself. As you make the effort God will bless and encourage you.

That said, if you need to streamline your study for some reason one week, the starred (*) questions would give you the bare bones of each lesson. Keep in mind, that's all it will be, bare bones. The studies are divided into three sections, as noted earlier. If you need even smaller chunks, you note the number of questions in the lesson and pace yourself accordingly.

The significance of the prophets writing was not so much their personal lives as it was their message. What are the truths that God wants to communicate to you and me about Himself and His purposes in our lives? What principles and promises do I find in these books that help me live my life today? Finally, God has left us a very clear blueprint regarding His plans for the future. The Minor Prophets are quoted some 90 times in Revelation alone!

At the end of this study are two timelines. One with the whole of Old Testament History in view; the second is intended for you to use as we study through the prophets. You will be able to add names of kings and prophets as we go along.

Historical Background

*1. What was God's purpose in calling out a nation for Himself?
   Deuteronomy 4: 6-8 and 32-39

2. When Israel entered the Promised Land, God gave them Judges. Who was the last judge and what happened?
   1 Samuel 8:1-9

3. Who were the kings during what is now called the United Kingdom? See Acts 13:20-22 and 1 Kings 2:1-3. Fill them in on your timeline.

   (1)_____
   (2)_____
   (3)_____

   After Solomon's death, his foolish son, Rehoboam, lost most of the kingdom to Jeroboam (from the tribe of Ephraim,) who established the northern kingdom of Israel. (2 Chronicles 10) A later king built the city of Samaria and it became the capital of northern Israel, sometimes called Ephraim. The southern Kingdom, made up mostly of the tribes of Judah and Benjamin, was called Judah and later Judea. Their capital was Jerusalem.

*4. There were many prophets throughout the history of Israel. Elijah and Elisha are two well-known prophets. (2 Kings 2) As we go through the study, we will want to put our prophets on a timeline, so we can clearly see when they were living and preaching and who would have been ruling during their lifetimes. That will help us understand the historical context. You have been provided with a chart on which you will add the prophet each week.

   Locate your Old Testament Timeline and the Minor Prophets Overview charts on pages 79-83. Can you put Elijah and Elisha in the Timeline?

Scriptural Context

5. Throughout the minor prophets, there are obscure references and symbolism relating to things that would have been common knowledge to the original readers/listeners. Understanding the historical context will help us understand these sometimes odd references.

   For Example: Joel 3:2 refers to the altars of Bethel, and Joel 4 to the "cows of Bashan." How does the following help you understand this in context?

   Jeroboam I : What did this king do to establish the northern kingdom?
   1 Kings 12:25-33

6. The New Testament reinforces the importance of the Minor Prophets for us. In Acts 2, Peter's first sermon is full of Old Testament references, as well as Stephen's sermon in Acts 7.

   After Jesus resurrection, He appears to two men. What was their conundrum and how did Jesus explain it to them?
   Luke 24:13-32

   What did Paul believe about the prophets? (Acts 24:14)

   Look at Paul's testimony in Acts 26. Restate Paul's message in your own words.
   Acts 26: 17, 18

   Acts 26:22, 23

   Another thing to keep in mind as we study the Minor Prophets is that we often have to figure out who is speaking! Sometimes it is the author speaking to God, or speaking to the people. Sometimes it is God speaking to the author or to the people. And sometimes it is God speaking to Jesus/king/Messiah/shepherd. Look for clues as you study.

*7. There are many overarching themes that can be followed across the centuries that the Minor Prophets ministered. God as creator, the heart, God's wrath, God's love, God's calling, God's Justice, etc. There is a strong emphasis on judgment, but watch for the mercy as well! It's always there. God is infinitely holy, infinitely merciful, infinitely just. All the time. Due to our limited understanding, certain attributes are expressed more at different times. I have made a page for you on "The Day of the Lord" (page 77) which is a major theme. As you find others, keep track of them to compare your findings with your class.

Personal Holiness

There are many things we cannot know for certain; even the dating of each minor prophet can be controversial. We want to keep in mind our purpose to know God better and be transformed into the image of His Son. As we focus on that and immerse ourselves in the Word, the prophet's call to personal holiness will become ours.

*8. The book of Hebrews is all about how the Old Testament is completed in the New. What does Hebrews 1:1-3 say about the prophets"

What does it say about Christ?

*9. Look at the following passages in Hebrews. What is the warning/or "let us"?
Hebrews 2:1-3

Hebrews 3:7-13

Hebrews 4:8-16

(What is this "rest"?)

*10. What is the ongoing message of Hebrews?
Hebrews 10:37-39

Hebrews 12:22-24 and 28, 29

How would you explain the relationship between the Old Testament and the New? What is the value of studying the Old Testament?

Each week there will be a memory verse. I challenge you and your class to memorize them together. Take the time to think about what the lesson means for your life today. How do the truths you learn affect the way you live, the way you treat others or the way you hope? God left us these books for a purpose; let's enjoy the journey of discovering a few of the reasons why!

"Let the Word of Christ dwell in you richly , with all wisdom teaching and admonishing one another with psalms and hymns and spiritual songs, singing with thankfulness in your hearts to God." Col. 3:16

Hosea, *"Salvation"*
Lesson 2

So let us know, let us press on to know the Lord. His going forth is as certain as the dawn. He will come to us like the rain, like the spring rain watering the earth. Hosea 6:3

1. Try to read the 14 chapters. It's always good to familiarize yourself with the territory before we go back and examine the issues!

Historical Background 782-725 B.C.

2. Who were the kings in Israel and Judah during Hosea's long years of ministry?
   Put them on your timeline.
   Hosea 1:1
   2 Kings chapters 14-17

   Kings in Judah   Kings in Israel

> *During the reign of **Jeroboam II**, Amos, Hosea, Joel and Micah were preaching in different places.*

After many decades of peace and prosperity for Israel, Egypt's world influence is waning and that of Assyria (Nineveh) is growing. Israel tried to form many alliances with Assyria, neighboring nations and Egypt.

> *Ephraim- Refers to the tribe of Israel that was one of Joseph's sons. It was used to refer to the Northern Kingdom of Israel. Jeroboam I, the first king of the Northern Kingdom was an Ephraimite, making this tribe central and influential in the northern kingdom.*

Scriptural Context

The book of Hosea is difficult to outline into neat and tidy compartments. It is an expression of the heart of God, which is so far beyond our comprehension that all we can do is break off bite size pieces and try to grasp what it is the Lord would have us learn today. Therefore, many of my "boxes" will require you to flip through the book, dig out those morsels of truth and hope as God graciously reveals His heart to us.

Chapter 1

*3. a. What is the assignment that God gives to Hosea? (1:2)

b. List the names of Hosea's three children and what those names mean.

c. "Yet." What is the promise that God makes? (1:10, 11)

Chapter 2

*4. a. Explain the picture/metaphor that God is making. Why is Israel the wife? (2:2) See also Hosea 11:1-4

b. What does she do?

c. What will God do? **Hosea 2:1-13**

d. Despite their sin, what hope does God give? **Hosea 2:14-20**

e. How do you reconcile that God is both punisher and rewarder?

5. Look at **Hosea 1:10 and 2:23**. What is God's promise to Israel? See also Isaiah 62:4, 5

Chapter 3

*6. What does God tell Hosea to do in this chapter?

What does this chapter reveal about the character of God?

Chapters 4-13

Questions 7-14. On the chart, (page 14) I have suggested three subjects I would like you to look for as we delve into these chapters. You can either do them one at a time, or look for all three as you go through each chapter. Don't be overwhelmed. Take your time and find the treasures that God has for YOU today.
You will look for:

God's complaint. Those things that have hurt God's heart.

*The Call. Those passages where God's heart calls to His children.

The Response. What is the response that God is looking for?
I have put a couple of references under each heading to get you started, but there are more!

God's Complaint	God's Character/Heart	What is God looking for?

Hosea Chapters 4-13	*Example:*
	  Hosea 10:12
	
	  Hosea 14:1, 2
		Example:
		  Hosea 5:15-6:3, 6

*15. Read Hosea 12:1. Can you explain why making this covenant was so wrong??

*16. In the following passages, what are some of the truths you find about God? What do you notice about Him? Add them to your chart.

Hosea 11:1, 4, 8, 9

Hosea 13:4

Personal Holiness

Chapter 14

*17. a. What is the call here? **Hosea 14:1,2a**

b. What is the desired response? 14:2b-3a

c. What is the truth? 14:3b-8

d. Once again, what is the call? 14:9

Have you experienced Jesus' rescue? Would you be willing to share your story with the class? Or maybe you need to let Him rescue you! ☺

*18. a. Who or what is "the Bride" in these days in which we live?

Ephesians 5:25-32

Revelation 19:7,8

b. As the Bride of Christ, what is our role in history? (Revelation 22:17)

19. Meditate on the memory verse. (Is there a command to obey? Promise to claim? Warning to heed? Something to give thanks for?)

Joel *"The Lord is God"*
Lesson 3

"Yet even now," declares the Lord, "Return to Me with all your heart...and rend your heart and not your garments. ...For the Lord is gracious and compassionate, Slow to anger and abounding in lovingkindness"Joel 2:12,13

*1. Read the Book. (3 chapters, you can do it! ☺)

Historical Background 830 B.C.

2. Look at 2 Chronicles 22:10-24:27 and answer the questions.
    a. What was going on in Judah just before Joash became king?

    b. What was unique about Joash's childhood and coronation?

    c. Why did things go well for Joash at first?

    d. What marked the second half of Joash's reign?

    e. Put any characters on your Timeline

Scriptural Context

Joel 1
3. a. To whom does Joel direct his message? **Joel 1:1-5**

    b. What has apparently occurred?

    c. How does Joel describe the invasion of locusts? **Joel 1:6, 7, 10-12**

*4. Often there is just no answer to the question "Why?" Simply the fact of the disaster. Joel doesn't ask why, but he knows what to do. Maybe he had read Psalm 73: 25 and 26 that morning?

How might these verses have encouraged him?

What does Joel teach us about responding to catastrophe?

> *A plague of locusts is not an uncommon thing in Palestine. Throughout history, they have returned to plague the nation. Joel uses the recent plague of locusts (chapter 1) to foreshadow the certain judgment that God will one day deliver. (Chapters 2 and 3) A partial fulfillment of this prophecy occurred with the coming of the Chaldeans in the year 605. As you study, see if you can discover why the Chaldeans invasion was only a partial fulfillment.*

*5. Before we go any further, we need to examine this phrase, **"the Day of the Lord."** Note the characteristics of the Day of the Lord as used in the different passages.

Joel 1:15

Joel 2:1, 2

Joel 2:11

Joel 2:31

Joel 3:14

Alluded to:
Joel 2:18

Joel 3:1

Joel 3:18

> **The Day of Yahweh, William P. Griffith, PhD.**
> *In the OT the concept of the Day of Yahweh was not fixed, but adaptable to whatever situation confronted the prophets. It is an expression, which is not as specific in the OT as it is in the NT and applies to multiple days of the Lord. Joel shows the greatest variety in his applications of the concept. The term was used against both God's people and against their enemies. It was used in relation to the events of his time in one place and to the distant future in another. Joel even quotes himself with different applications!*

So we see that "the day of the Lord" is much more than a 24 hour period. It might be considered as a grouping of events that will culminate world history. Joel gives us an unfolding order of events. These events will have near and far fulfillments. This is called the Principle of Double Reference.

6. **Joel 2:1-11** describes the first three events. Look at the suggested cross-references. Perhaps you can find others.

Event		Cross References
I. _____ **Joel 2:1**		Revelation 8:6
II. _____ **Joel 2:2-10**		Revelation 9:1-11
III. _____ **Joel 2:11**		Revelation 19:11-16

7. a. In **Joel 2:12-29,** we have an interlude. What is it about? Why is it there?

   b. What response is God looking for? **Joel 2:12, 13, 15-17**

*8. a. Look at **Joel 2:18-32**. What is the Lord's response to their repentance?

b. Stop a minute. What kind of God is this who sends devastation and yet in practically the same breath offers staggering blessings? Write down everything we can know about Him from **chapter 2**.

```
┌─────────────────────────────────────────────────────┐
│                                                     │
│                                                     │
│                                                     │
│                                                     │
│                                                     │
└─────────────────────────────────────────────────────┘
```

9. Peter saw something when he quoted **Joel 2:28, 29** in Acts 2:17-21. Do you think this was a partial or complete fulfillment of the prophecy? Why or why not?

          Event   **Cross References**

10. IV._____ **Joel 3:1, 2**   Revelation 14:14-20

    What is to happen? Where? Joel 3:9-15

    What is God's purpose?

    Joel 2:27

    Joel 3:17

    Isaiah 11:9, 10

    Isaiah 56:7

11. V._____ **Joel 3:17**   Revelation 19:15

    What will characterize Christ's reign? (Joel 3:17)

Personal Holiness

The Holy God will one day dwell in Zion and rule His kingdom on earth. I would like us to think about His kingdom today, and our role in it. The Holy God of the Universe dwells in the believer! Each of us is a Tabernacle where God can dwell; together we make the church, His Body in the world. God is Holy. Holiness should therefore characterize our lives.

*12. a. When I am frustrated by the apparent lack of justice in the world, what truth from this book can I remember that will help to put things in perspective?

See also:
John 3:18

Revelation 16:7

   b. How can we reflect God's holiness in our own day-to-day worlds? (Perhaps share how you have seen holiness displayed in someone else's life.)

*13. In addition to what you found in chapter 2, add anything else you find in this book that reveals the character of God. Be sure to note the reference.

*14. Meditate on the memory verse. (Is there a command to obey? Promise to claim? Warning to heed? Something to give thanks for?)

Amos, "Burden Bearer"
Lesson 4

"Take away from Me the noise of your songs; I will not even listen to the sound of your harps. But let justice roll down like waters and righteousness like an ever flowing stream. Amos 5:23, 24

1. It can't be avoided. If we are going to do this right, we'll need to read the whole book. Ask the Father to reveal Himself to you!

Historical Background 760-750 B. C.

2. Who was Amos? (**Amos 1:1 and 7:14, 15**)

3. Who was Jeroboam II? 2 Kings 14:23, 24

   Who was king in Judah? 2 Kings 15:1, 2

4. What do you see as the social context? (Amos 5:1-13 and 6:1, 4-6)

   Place any characters or events on your Timeline.

> *During this century, both Judah and Israel had reached political and military heights. Peace reigned and business was flourishing. Even Assyria was quiet after the national repentance that took place under the preaching of Jonah. Despite the prosperous exterior, we'll see what Amos has to reveal beneath the façade.*

Scriptural Content

Amos is a very interesting book, with many insights and lessons for us today. But like most Old Testament prophets, their eastern thought processes are more circular, which makes them seem complicated to our linear thinking western minds. I have tried to ask questions that will help us put it all together, but the scriptures I give are not exhaustive. Please feel free to add more, as it will also add to your understanding of what God wants to teach us through this book.

*5. One of the things about God that we see in the Old Testament is that He always makes clear *why* He does things.

   a. Why is God angry with Judah and Israel?
      Amos 3:2

3:9,10

4:4-6, 8

5:21-23

6:12,13

Just as the average housewife in seventh century Israel didn't always know why God was doing what He did, today, we 21st century believers can't always see the "why" behind all the things God does.

b. What can we do when life seems to explode? Hebrews 13:5-8

6. a. Why was God so unhappy with His people? **Amos 4:6, 8, 9, 10, 11.**

b. What are some of the expectations/desires that God has for His people?

Amos 5:4-6

5:14, 15

5:24

c. Why should God expect this? Amos 4:13

*7. Glance through **chapters 1-5**, and write down all you can find that is true about God. I like to mark these in yellow.

*8. a. **Amos 4:1** God makes a very harsh statement. What does He call the women of Samaria?

   b. I think it behooves us to consider our role as women before God. What was our curse? Genesis 3:16 (consider what it means that our natural desire is to rule our husbands.)

   c. What are some of the harsh realities taught about women in the New Testament?
   1 Corinthians 11, 8, 9

   2 Corinthians 11:3

   1 Timothy 2:12-14

   d. To balance this, what do we see is Jesus' attitude (and the Father's) towards women? (I put only a couple of examples, there are hundreds.)

   Luke 10:38-42

   John 20:11-17 *(Jesus is busy—20:17, yet He pauses, He sees her, He comforts her.)*

   Genesis 16:13

   Genesis 21:17

*9. As women, how do we uniquely reflect the character of God?

As wives, mothers and friends, we are very influential people. What influence are you having on your home and/or workplace?

How can we improve the influence we make? (Luke 6:45, and Luke 8: 15)

10. God makes a lot of promises in Amos, some for judgment and some for restoration. In these two passages, see what you can find under each heading.
   Amos 8:7-14
   Amos 9:8-15

   Promises for Judgment   Promises for Restoration

*11. a. What is a plumb line, and what do you think God wants to communicate with this illustration? **Amos 7:7-9**

   b. We know that God does not change. So what is the plumb line for our life? (Hebrews 4:12)

12. Amos has some things to say about the Day of the Lord. What do you learn? Add them to your chart on The Day of the Lord. (Page 77.)
   Amos 5:18-20

*13. What truths about God do you find in **Chapters 6-9**?

Personal Holiness

*14. a. Consider the word "justice" in the following verses.

  Amos 5:7

  Amos 5:15

  Amos 5:24

  Amos 6:12

  b. Where do we find Justice today? Matthew 12:18-21

Pray about how you can express this hope in your sphere of influence.

*15. Look again at our memory verse at the top of the lesson.

  a. What do you see as your role in the body of Christ?

  b. How do you reflect the character of God in your world?

  c. Why is it important for us as women to keep our focus on the plumb line?

  d. Meditate on the memory verse.
  (Is there a command to obey? Promise to claim? Warning to heed? Something to give thanks for?)

Obadiah/ Jonah /Nahum
Lesson 5

The Lord is good, a stronghold in the day of trouble,
And He knows those who take refuge in Him.   Nahum 1:7

Before you panic, let me just say I know it seems like a lot for one week. It is. However, due to time constraints, I stuck these three prophets together. As we study, look for why I did that. I have tried to break it down for you into bite size bits, but if it still overwhelms you **simply choose one*** of them to study, and come to class ready to share your insights and learn from the others.

*In all three books we will be looking especially at **the character of God** that is revealed. If you do nothing else, find that.*

I have left the books in chronological order, but honestly, once you understand Nahum, you will understand Jonah better. We will do our timeline together in class.

Obadiah, *"Servant/worshiper of the Lord"*

1. Read the book/chapter.

    Obadiah means "Servant of the Lord." The name is found many times in the OT and refers to many different people. Opinions differ dramatically on the date of this book.

2. Obadiah's prophecy is against Edom. Who were these guys?
Genesis 25:19-34

    Genesis 36:9

    Numbers 20:14-21

    2 Kings 8:20-22

3. What does Obadiah cite as God's specific complaint against Edom at this time?

    Obadiah 10-14 (see Psalm 137:7)

*4. a. What was the great sin of Edom?
      Obadiah 3

b. Would you say pride is still a problem today? What are some ways it manifests itself?

c. How can we deal with pride in our own lives?

*5. a. "But God." What is the hope that God gives? **Obadiah 17-21**

b. What is one long-standing promise of God? Genesis 12:3

> **Nineveh**: *Capital city of Assyria, Nineveh dominated the Ancient Near East for most of 900 to 612 B.C. 8 miles in circumference, the city walls were at least 50 feet high and wide enough for three chariots to ride abreast. The walls enclosed some 1,700 acres. Around the wall were 15 gates with 1,500 huge watch/defense towers. A river and moat enclosed the city, which had many parks, lakes and water features. What is known of the palace covered three large city blocks. Many sculpted relief's from the palace depicting the grandeur of the kingdom, and including the conquest of Lachish, can be seen at the British Museum. Ashurbanipal's library was discovered with over 1500 texts, including Senacharib's account of his conquest of Judah in 701. Hezekiah is even mentioned by name! The Assyrians were extraordinary artists, and what little is left is breathtaking.*

Jonah, *"Dove"*

*6. Most of us are familiar with the story of Jonah; whole studies have been written on this little book. Today, let's just look at a couple of things. Read the four little chapters and write down your first impressions. What's the book about, really?

7. According to 2 Kings 14:25, Jonah lived during the long and prosperous reign of Jeroboam II, placing him in the northern kingdom around 760-770 B.C. Jewish tradition says Jonah was the son of the widow of Zarephath. 1 Kings 17: 8-24. Who knows??

a. Place Jonah and any other pertinent information on your timeline.(page 81)

b. Who were the Ninevites, and why do you think Jonah had such an aversion to going to them?

8. We'll leave the ramifications of Jonah's unique "cruise" for another time. Think about Jonah as a prophet, his message and his audience.

a. What did Jonah do when he had exhausted all his own resources and "escape options? Chapter 2

b. What was unique about Jonah's "method of evangelism?" **Jonah 3:1-4**

What might be the reaction if this method were employed today?

What was Nineveh's reaction to the message? **Jonah 3:5-9**

What was God's response to that? **Jonah 3:10**

*9. What conclusions can you draw about the character of God from the book of Jonah?
Chapter:

1.	2.	3.	4.

Nahum, *"Comfort, Consolation"*

Don't worry. We'll come back to Micah! For now skip over to Nahum and read the three little chapters in one sitting.

Because Nineveh is seen as a powerful nation in this book, it is thought to have been written before the death of Ashurbanipal in 626 B.C., after which Assyria's power declined rapidly. No-Ammon (Thebes/Egypt) 3:8-10, was destroyed by Ashurbanipal between 663-662. The suggested date for the book is during the reign of Manasseh 695-642. 2 Kings 21:1-18

   *10. 100 years after Jonah, what is the spiritual state of Nineveh?
      Nahum 1:11
          3:1-4

   *11. The name Nahum means consolation or comforter. How do you see God consoling and comforting in this book?

      Notice the pattern in **Nahum 1:1-2:3**. What do you see about the character/person of God?

      What does it mean that God is jealous? (Nahum 1:2)

   12. How does **Nahum 1:15-2:2** fit in with the rest of the book?

      What is the good news of peace? (Ephesians 2:14)

   13. Apparently, unlike Jonah, Nahum didn't actually go to Nineveh, but prophesied rather from Judah. What was God's purpose in that do you think? What do you think Nahum/God hoped his audience would apply?

> *Nineveh should have been able to withstand a twenty-year siege. In 612, after three months Nahum 1:8 was fulfilled when the Tigress overflowed and washed away part of the walls, allowing the Babylonians to enter.*

Personal Holiness

*14. What do Obadiah, Jonah and Nahum have in common?

Of twelve minor prophets, ¼ are dedicated to non-Jewish nations. Why do you think that is?

*15. What did God desire to do through the nation of Israel? Deuteronomy 3:6-8 and 4:32-39

What is God's attitude toward the nations? (See Acts 17:30 and Revelation 14:6, 7)

*16 Are there any principles and/or promises from these three books that we can glean for our 21st century lives?

What about exhortations? How about Matthew 5:16, and Romans 10:1, 12-15? Can you think of any others?

17. What stands out to you about the character of God as seen in these books?

    What challenges you?

    What comforts/consoles you?

18. Meditate on the memory verse.
    (Is there a command to obey? Promise to claim? Warning to heed? Something to give thanks for?)

Micah *"Who is like Jehovah"*
Lesson 6

But as for me, I will watch expectantly for the Lord; I will wait for the God of my salvation. My God will hear me. Do not rejoice over me, O my enemy. Though I fall I will rise; though I dwell in darkness, the Lord is a light for me.
Micah 7:7, 8

Historical Background
Anytime between 740 and 695

1. According to Micah 1:1, what do we know about Micah and his times?

2. Micah marks the center of the Twelve Books, making it pivotal in Hebrew literature. Look at <u>some</u> of the cross-references and try to put what you can on your timeline. (page 81)
   2 Kings 15:8-20

   2 Chronicles 27-32

   Isaiah 7-8

   Jeremiah 26:17-19

   What was going on in the world during this time?

Scriptural Context

As you read through the book once again remember you will see the near and far prophecies all mixed together. Micah sees all of history. At one moment the prophet will be speaking; at the next God speaks. Remember, we can't expect "linear thinking" (western style) in a Hebrew context!

3. Micah's book can be broken up into three sections, which we will look at one by one. See if you can give each one a title. What does each section begin with?
   Micah 1:2
       3:1
       6:1

I.   **Micah 1:2-2:13** _____
                    Title

4. **Micah 1:2-16.** What is God's complaint and to whom is He specifically speaking?

*5. **Micah 2:1-13.** As God continues the list of infractions, what hope do you see in the middle of it all?

*6. What Truths about God do you find in Micah 1 and 2?

```

```

II.   **Micah 3:1-5:15** _____
                     Title

Chapter 3.

* 7. Who specifically is God calling on the carpet?

While we're on this subject, what does the New Testament have to say about leaders? See Hebrews 13:17.

8. Look at **Micah 3:4.** When does God <u>not</u> hear us?
(Isaiah 59:1, 2; James 4:1-4; Psalm 66:18)

Chapter 4 Watch out for the "now" and "then" passages. Be ready to discuss which is which and where they might fit on your *Extended Time Line*.

9. **Micah 4:11-13** says "Now," but it also has a future. Do you know what they are?

   "Now"   "Future"

   2 Kings 17:1-9   Revelation 14:14-16

Chapter 5. Here we have more mixed prophecies.

10. **Micah 5:1-3** has a "nearer" prophesy. Can you find the New Testament fulfillment?

    Micah 5:3b-9 says "then," what will happen?

11. **Micah 5:10-15** Says "In that day." What is to be expected? (Revelation 16:14; 17:1, 2, 14; 18:1-24; 19:15)

* 12. What Truths about God do you find in **Micah 3-5**

III. Micah 6, 7 _____
Title

Chapter 6. These last two chapters are almost like a conversation between Micah and God. The transitions aren't as important as what we take away from it all.

* 13. **Micah 6:1,2.** "Hear, Listen." What does God want them to remember? Why?

    Why is "remember" a theme in Scripture? What is something you need to "remember?

14. **Micah 6:5.** Who were Baalam and Balak? This was a familiar story to Micah's audience. Just mentioning the names brought to mind all the lessons and principles God intended them to learn. We may have to catch up a little!
(Numbers 22 and Deuteronomy 23:5)

    Why is the "sin of Baalam" so pertinent for us today?
    2 Peter 2:15

    Jude 1:11

    Revelation 2:14

*15. **Micah 6:6-8.** So what does worship look like? (What does God expect of us?)

    <u>Old Testament Corroboration</u>   <u>New Testament</u>
    Deuteronomy 10:12

    Psalm 51:16,17

    Isaiah 66:2

Lest we think all these admonishments in Micah are only for the "unsaved," we can see from Micah 6:4 that the context is to an *already ransomed* people. As Christians, why might all these warnings still be viable today?

Chapter 7

*16. Despite the circumstances (Micah 7:1-6), I love how Micah says, "but as for me." What is his determination? **Micah 7:7-9**

Micah 7:10-20. Then, what is the future hope that is revealed?

*17. What Truths about God do you find in Micah 6 and 7?

Personal Holiness

*18 Think about the circumstances surrounding your life. How do you want to respond to God today as you "dwell in the land?" (Psalm 37:3)

19. What have you seen in this book that most encourages and or challenges you this week? (You might look at the boxes we created on Truths about God.)

20. Meditate on the memory verse.
    (Is there a command to obey? Promise to claim? Warning to heed? Something to give thanks for?)

Zephaniah- *"Yahweh has hidden/protected"*
Lesson 7

The Lord your God is in your midst, a victorious warrior. He will exult over you with joy, He will be quiet in His love, He will rejoice over you with shouts of joy.
Zephaniah 3:17

Historical Background 640-609

1. Let's look at the back-story to Zephaniah. Fill in the chart and answer the question, what was the social and political climate for most of the 50 years preceding the time of Zephaniah? Fill in anything you can on your timeline. (page 81)

   Who was the king?   What was his "epitaph"?
   2 Kings 21:1-6, 16

   _____

   2 Kings 21:19-26

   _____

   2 Kings 22   2 Kings 23:24, 25

> *It is thought that Zephaniah was born during the bloody reign of Manasseh. (Tradition holds that it was Manasseh who had Isaiah killed.) As we consider the social and political climate at the time 8-year-old Josiah takes the throne, it is interesting to think that perhaps Zephaniah was influential in the young boys life. (Zeph 1:1)*

2. Which nation is the threat at the time Zephaniah writes? Zeph. 2:13

> **Did You Know? (from the Archaelogical Bible)**
> - *Incense to pagan deities was often burned on rooftops. (see Isa 15:3; Jer 1:16) and the kings of Judah had gone so far as to erect pagan altars on the roof of the palace in Jerusalem. Zeph 1:5)*
> - *There was evidently a general and widespread pagan idea that the threshold of a home, temple or other building was the dwelling place of spirits. (Zeph 1:9) See also 1 Samuel 5:1-6.*
> - *Nineveh was destroyed in 619 B.C. and its location was later forgotten –until archaeologists discovered it in 1845 A.D. (Zeph 2:13)*

Scriptural Context

*3. Look at **Zephaniah 1:2-13**.
   a. Why is God upset?

   b. What is His promise?

   c. What does God make clear in Zephaniah 1:6,12?

4. Read **Zephaniah 1:14-18** and write down what it describes about **the Day of the Lord.**

*5. Now read **Zephaniah 2**.
   a. What is happening in this chapter?

   b. What is the warning?

   c. What is the hope?

6. Who are the "remnant"? Zephaniah mentions them in 2:7 and 9 and again in 3:13.

> **Still Curious?** Check out these verses that mention "**the remnant.**" Who do you conclude the remnant is?
>
> In the Minor Prophets
> Micah 2:12
>   4:7
>   5: 7, 8
>   7:18
> Zechariah 8:6-13
>   9:7
>
> In Major Prophets
> Isaiah 10:20-22
>   11:11-16
>   37:31, 32
> Jeremiah 23:3-6
>   50:17-20
> Ezekiel 6:8-10

*7. In **Zephaniah 3,** we have multiple references to "that day" and "that time."
   a. According to Zephaniah 3:8-20 what will happen?

   b. What does God desire? Zephaniah 3:7,8

   c. How do you think this relates to today? (See 2 Peter 3:10-13)

*8. Note down any truths you find about God from **Zephaniah Chapter 3**.

I see so many things happening on "The Day of the Lord." (Remember our explanation in Lesson 3, page 19?) There are so many layers of fulfillment! Can you locate any "fulfillments," and what is yet future? Pursue your own questions by following cross-references. Bring your findings to class.

Personal Holiness

*9. a. What is the call in **Zephaniah 3:14**?

b. Explain why that call is for me as well as the people living in Zephaniah's day.

*10. **Zephaniah 3:15-20** why can I (should I) rejoice?

*11. Meditate on the memory verse.
(Is there a command to obey? Promise to claim? Warning to heed? Something to give thanks for?)

Habakkuk, *"One Who Embraces"* (possibly)
Lesson 8

For the vision is yet for the appointed time; It hastens toward the goal and it will not fail. Though it tarries, wait for it; For it will certainly come, it will not delay. Habakkuk 2:3

Historical Background possibly 609-608

1. Habakkuk lived at the same time as Jeremiah, Ezekiel, Daniel and Zephaniah. Let's find the context of his times. Read 2 Kings 22 and 23. Put them on your timeline. (page 81)

2. How long did Josiah rule? What were some of the reforms he instituted?

   What was his epitaph? 2 Kings 23:25

> *During these years, the power of Babylon is rising. Nabopolassar (Nebuchadnezzar's dad) captured Nineveh and defeated the Assyrians in 612 B.C. Soon the Babylonians (or Chaldeans as Habakkuk calls them), consolidated their power and began to move westward toward Egypt, the competing world power in that day.*
>
> *Who knows what Josiah was thinking, but he decided to confront Pharaoh Neco and his armies as they rode to meet the Babylonian army. Josiah was killed at the Megiddo pass in 609 B.C. Four years later the Egyptians are defeated and Judea comes under the control and authority of Nebuchadnezzar. That year, 605, Daniel and his friends are taken as hostages to Babylon.*

3. Things happened pretty quickly after that. What happened after Josiah's death?
   2 Kings 23:31-35

Scriptural Context

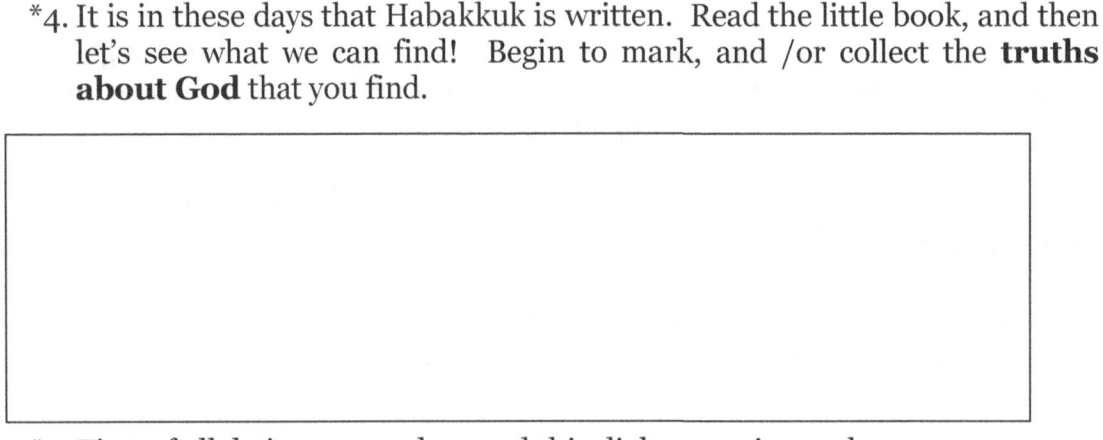

*4. It is in these days that Habakkuk is written. Read the little book, and then let's see what we can find! Begin to mark, and /or collect the **truths about God** that you find.

[   ]

*5. First of all, let's try to understand this dialogue going on between Habakkuk and God.
What does **Habakkuk say in 1:2-4**

How does God respond to him? **Habakkuk 1:5-11**

Now, in **1:12-2:2 Habakkuk** speaks again. What is he saying?

It's the question of the ages isn't it? How can a Holy God, (whose goodness is implied) use unholy tools to affect His purposes? (We'll come back to this question at the end of our study.)

*6. What do you observe about the Lord's answer? **Habakkuk 2:2-20**

Several truths about God stand out. What are they, why would God use these particular things right then? (Cross references: Revelation 16:6,7 and 19:1,2)

7. **Habakkuk 2:3** refers to a "vision." What does it say, and what might it refer to? Look at some of the cross-references for ideas.

Hab. 2:4 see Zechariah 14:9 and Revelation 19:11-16

For Hab. 2:20 see Revelation 8:1

*8. **Habakkuk 2:4** is a much quoted verse in the New Testament. Look at the context in one or two of the cross-references. How and why is it quoted? Why is it such a significant verse? Be ready to discuss what this verse actually means, what it implies, and what it looks like for us today.

Acts 13:41

Romans 1:17

Galatians 3:11

Hebrews 10:38f

*9. I would also like to consider the example of Abraham. Romans 4:3 and 20, 21. What does it say about him?

Look at Romans 3:21-26
First of all, what is righteousness? (I see it 4 times in the passage!)

Why was it "manifested, demonstrated?

What is accomplished and for whom?

Explain how these Old and New Testament references relate to each other.

*10. **Chapter 3** is clearly stated, a prayer. *(It is significant to understand the stated style in which it's written. Shigioneth; wild, enthusiastic, triumphal.)*

Habakkuk 3:16-19

What does Habukkuk believe about God? What is his response to his circumstances?

Personal Holiness

*11. What can you learn from Habakkuk about responding to your own circumstances?

What is the commitment of YOUR heart?

12. Think back to our "question of the ages." (#5 page 46) Does God answer the question in this book?

If you say "yes", how does He answer it?

If you say "no", why do you think not?

13. Meditate on the Memory Verse.
    (Is there a command to obey? Promise to claim? Warning to heed? Something to give thanks for?)

Did you know!!

The Chaldeans served the god Marduk (often represented by a bull). From tablets discovered in Ur, there is a creation story about him. He was one of many gods, but very rambunctious. He loved to throw dust on the sea (Tiamat his great grandma). This annoys the other gods, who can't find a champion to fight for them against him, so they ask Marduk himself to be their champion, and defeat Tiamat. (Sorry, I can't follow the logic either.) Anyway, Marduk says he will be their champion if they will serve him. Deal. So after a long (and wordy) battle, Marduk defeats his great grandma. He uses a net and arrows, and finally splits open her body, "like a dying fish." From that he creates the heavens and the earth. He proposes to build the great city Babylon, especially the main temple Esaglia as a place for the gods to go up and down between the worlds. The city is dedicated with great ceremony and all Marduk's 50 (!) names are proclaimed.

I would suggest this story was common knowledge in Habukkuk's day. Can you find anything in the book that speaks to this counterfeit?

Haggai, *"Festal One"*
Lesson 9

"But now take courage" declares the Lord, "take courage and work, for I am with you," declares the Lord of Hosts.   Haggai 2:3

Historical Background 520 B.C. (second year of Darius)
We now jump some 100 years in history, so it's pretty important that we fill in the gap. We have skipped the prophets Jeremiah, Ezekiel and Daniel who fit into this time frame. Fill in whatever you can on your timeline. (page 81)

*1. Use the passages to help you understand *"What Happened?"*
Jeremiah 38: 17-23

Jeremiah 39: 1-10

Jeremiah 40:1-6

2 Chronicles 36:11-23

Ezra 2:64

Ezra 3:8, 9

Ezra 4:1-4

Scriptural Context
Construction on the temple has been halted for 16 years. The book contains many "principles" (truths to live by).

2. Who was Zerubbable? See 1 2 Kings 24:8-17.

*3. **Haggai 1:1-15**
What was the problem that Haggai saw? What were the people saying? (1:2)

What do you see as the people's priorities? (1:4)

What is the instruction that the Lord gives?

What did God expect from them? (1:8-11)

How do the people respond? (1:12, 14)

How does the Lord encourage them? (1:13)

What principle do you see in this portion?

*4. Haggai 2:1-9
After a month, why were the people discouraged? (2:3)

What does the Lord say to them? (2:4)

What is the perspective that God wants them to see? (See also Hebrews 12:26, 27)

What principle do you see in this section?

*5. Haggai 2:10-19
What's going on here and why is it a problem?

Despite their sinfulness, what does the Lord say to them? (2:14-19)

What is the principle in this section?

*6. Haggai 2:20-23

What principle do you see?

7. Look over the two chapters of Haggai. Note any **truths you see about God.** (Remember to put the reference.)

```
┌─────────────────────────────────────────────┐
│                                             │
│                                             │
│                                             │
│                                             │
│                                             │
└─────────────────────────────────────────────┘
```

Personal Holiness

*8. What were David's priorities and how did he maintain them? Let's look at Psalm 119 and see what we can discover.

Read Psalm 119: 1-16.

What do you observe about David's heart?

What are the promises?

Are there any examples I can follow?

Can you find any truths about God?

What are your priorities and how do you plan to maintain them "until that day?"

9. Meditate on the Memory Verse.
    (Is there a command to obey? Promise to claim? Warning to heed? Something to give thanks for?)

(If you have extra time this week, you might want to begin the next lesson on Zechariah which is a bit longer than usual.)

If you do not already have a Bible-reading plan, I would like to challenge you to begin one. God's Word is our only compass in this stormy world. He has promised to be with us, to guide us, to dwell in us, but too often we are too busy "building our houses" to listen or even notice His hand. Take a few minutes and think honestly with the Lord.
What would you like Him to find you doing at the end of your life's journey?

Zechariah, *"The Lord Remembers"*
Part 1 Messiah as Servant
Lesson 10

"Not by might, nor by power, but by My Spirit." Says the Lord. Zechariah 4:6

Zechariah means "Jehovah remembers." The Lord remembers His people, His promises and His purposes.

Historical Background 520 B.C.

Zechariah was born in Babylonia and returned with the first group of exiles right after Cyrus gave his decree. Construction on the Temple began immediately, but because of opposition, building was halted for sixteen years. In Haggai, we saw how the people had become distracted during this time and Zechariah and Haggai together encouraged the people to believe God and press on putting first things first.

After Isaiah, Zechariah tells us more about the Messiah than any other book. Zechariah "saw" Jesus coming, both times, first as a Servant and also as a King. As you read this book, you will see the prophecies are all mixed up (see Zech 9:7-10 for an example). No wonder the Jewish leaders in Jesus' day had a hard time recognizing the Messiah! As we study, the trick will be to recognize where, in the grand scheme of things, the different prophecies go. By this time in your study of the Minor Prophets, you should be familiar with this. Keep in mind, discerning the meaning of prophecies might be a "flexible endeavor," but we can always look for non-negotiable promises and principles to live our lives by.

This is a difficult study on many levels. Let me encourage you, do what you can. Push yourself just a little bit further. I have not given exhaustive cross-references; if you more have questions, follow the cross-references listed for each verse in your Bible. Some might find it easier to look up the cross-references on Biblegateway.com. Personally, I like finding them in my Bible, and being able to mark them, but it is an option. I have tried to **bold** the key cross-references for those with time constraints.

Scriptural Context

Zechariah grew up in Babylonia, where symbolism was the order of the day. Much like it is today! (Insurance companies have figured this out, think gecko and duck.) So Zechariah's symbolism was not weird to his audience like it is to us. It will really help if you take a few minutes and make sure you understand the meaning of a few of the different symbols.

Using the cross-references as a guide, briefly state what each symbol means.

*1. <u>The Branch</u>, Zechariah 3:8, 9; 6:11-13

    Jeremiah 23:5, 6

    Jeremiah 33:15

    Isaiah 4:2-4

    Isaiah 11:1-5

    Isaiah 53:2

    Revelation 5:5

*2. <u>Seven Eyes</u>, Zechariah 3:9; 4:10

    Prov.15: 3

    Jeremiah 16:17

    Revelation 1:4

    Revelation 5:6

*3. <u>Stone</u>,   Zechariah 3:9, 4; 7, 12:3

Exodus 17:6 and (37 years later) Numbers 20: 8-12

Isaiah 28:16

Daniel 2;34, 35

Acts 4:11, 12

Revelation 2:17

*4. <u>Lampstand</u>, Zechariah 4:2

Exodus 25:31-40

Matthew 5:14-16

Philippians 2:15,16

Revelation 1:20 and 2:5

*5. <u>Olive Trees</u>, Zechariah 4:3,11 and 14

Romans 11:17-18

Revelation 11:4

6-13. In Zechariah 1-6, the author receives a series of visions, apparently on the same night. As you look at them, think about Zechariah's context, and also think about the big picture context. What might they mean? Jot down your ideas, and add any cross-references you come up with. *(Do try and think of your own meaning. Commentators have a vast array of ideas. We'll leave the definitive answer for when we can ask Jesus!)*

Vision Briefly Stated	Possible Meanings	Cross References
(1) **Zechariah 1:7-17**		*(Look for these in the margin of your Bible)*

_____

(2) **Zechariah 1:18-21**
Craftsmen, carpenters, blacksmith, stoneworker, metalworker, woodworker. Same word used for all.

_____

(3) **Zechariah 2:1-13**

_____

*(4) **Zechariah 3:1-10**

_____

*(5) **Zechariah 4:1-14**

Vision Briefly Stated	Possible Meanings	Cross References

(6) Zechariah 5:1-4

_____

(7) Zechariah 5:5-11

_____

(8) Zechariah 6: 1-8

Zechariah 7 and 8

Read these two chapters, which contain special messages from Zechariah.

*14. What do these tell us about God? (What is He like? What does He want/desire/expect?)

In chapter 8, what are the promises God makes?

Zechariah 9-11 *mostly* deals with the Messiah's first coming as a Servant.

15. *However*, look at **Zechariah 9:7-10.** It is like a microcosm of the book in that it holds the whole scope of history in four verses. Can you unravel those prophecies and place them on your timeline?

*7. "And I will remove their blood from their mouth
and their detestable things from between their teeth.
Then they also will be a remnant for our God,
and be like a clan in Judah. And Ekron like a Jebusite.*

*8. But I will camp around My house because of an army,
Because of him who passes by and returns;
and no oppressor will pass over them anymore,
for now I have seen with My eyes.*

*9. Rejoice greatly, O daughter of Zion!
Shout in triumph (vindicated and victorious) O daughter of Jerusalem!
Behold your king is coming to you;
He is just and endowed with salvation,
Humble and mounted on a donkey.
Even on a colt. The foal of a donkey.*

*10. I will cut off the chariot from Ephraim,
and the horse from Jerusalem;
and the bow of war will be cut off.
and He will speak peace to the nations;
and His dominion will be from sea to sea,
and from the River to the ends of the earth.*

Question numbers 16, 17, 18. Summarize briefly the contents of each chapter. Note any cross-references you come up with.

Chapter Contents	Cross-References/Notes
Chapter 9	
Chapter 10	
Chapter 11	

Personal Holiness

*19. According to what you have studied this week, how does God remember:

His People?

His Promise?

His Purpose?

How will you respond to God this week? What is the challenge you see before you?

20. Meditate on the Memory Verse.
    (Is there a command to obey? Promise to claim? Warning to heed? Something to give thanks for?)

Zechariah
Part 2 Messiah as King
Lesson 11

"And the Lord will be king over all the earth, in that day the Lord will be the only one, and His name the only one. Zechariah 14:9

Even though it cannot be cleanly divided, the book of Zechariah definitely shows us both comings/advents of the Messiah. No wonder the Jewish leaders were confused! Even with our Complete Scripture perspective it is sometimes difficult to sort out. Deut. 29:29 says, "The secret things belong to the Lord our God, but *the things revealed* belong to us and to our sons forever, that we may observe all the words of this law." The problem is, sometimes even the things revealed become muddled!

*1. As you read **Zechariah 12-14,** you will notice the change in tempo. And just in case we miss it, the phrase "in that day" is repeated some 17 times! Read all three chapters and then come back and answer the questions. I think you can expect a lively class discussion. Commentators are all over the map!

Zechariah 12

*2. Look at **Zechariah 12:1**. As we move to the Messiah as King, what does this verse tell us about God?

3. Zechariah 12:9. What will happen? Check out *a few* of the cross-references listed, and try to place this on your timeline.

Isaiah 63:1-6

Micah 5:5-15

Matthew 24:15-21

Revelation 12:13-15

    13:7

    16:13-16

    19:19

Zechariah 13

***4.** What does this chapter say about a fountain?

Can you find any references that explain this?

5. What does this chapter tell us about false prophets? (Hint. 13:6 the word "friends" can also be translated "lovers" / fellow idolaters.)

Zechariah 14

Question numbers 6, 7, 8. This chapter is rich with detail. **Choose at least three** of the suggested "trails" and discover more about each one. Perhaps there is one I missed? Follow it by hunting up cross references and bring your findings to share with the class. Mark any of these things on your timeline.
* (*If you are doing the bulleted pathway, choose one.*)

Gather the nations (14:1)

"The rest of the people will not be cut off" (14:2)

The Lord will go forth and fight. (14:3)

His feet will stand on the Mount of Olives (14:4)

Mount of Olives split (14:4)

You will flee (14:5)

Then the Lord will come and all His holy ones with Him. (14:5)

Neither day nor night (14: 6,7)

Living waters flow out of Jerusalem (14:8)

*9. What do we learn about "that day" when the Lord will be king? **Zechariah 14:9-11**

10. What will happen to those who go to war against the Lord? **Zechariah 14:12-15**.

(Notice how this portion is "book-ended." See Zech. 12:9 question number 3.) Why is that do you think?

Then, **Zechariah 14:16-21**, when is this? (14:11)

What will the nations do?

> **What is the Feast of Booths? Zechariah 14:16**
> *Also called the Feast of Tabernacles or Sukkoth, it took place five days after the Day of Atonement. (Numbers 29:12-40) The people "camped out" in small huts built of branches on the roofs of their houses. The idea was to remember their time as wanderers in the wilderness for forty years. (Lev. 23:43) This joyous week was a time of final celebration and thanksgiving for the year's harvest. (Duet. 16:14,15) As the seventh and last annual feast, the Feast of Booths also represented the Sabbath principle. The feast also looks forward to the coming eternal rest in the holy city when "the tabernacle of God is with men, and He will dwell with them and they shall be His people." Revelation 21:3 and Zechariah 14:16*

Personal Holiness

God remembers His people, His promise, His purpose.

*11. What do you need to remember about your God today?

What promise has He given you that you need to believe?

What purpose has He given you that you need to walk in?

*12. Glance back over these two lessons on Zechariah. What has stood out to you about:

The character of God?

The message of Zechariah?

13. Meditate on the memory verse.
    (Is there a command to obey? Promise to claim? Warning to heed?
    Something to give thanks for?)

Malachi, *"My Messenger"*
Lesson 12

Bring the whole tithe into the storehouse, so that there may be food in My house, and test Me now in this," says the Lord of hosts, "if I will not open for you the windows of heaven and pour out for you a blessing until it overflows."
Malachi 3:10

Historical Background
433-425

1. Malachi lends itself to a summary of the Minor Prophets. As you study, note any "echoes" that you find from earlier books. Take a minute to look back over the historical context of this time. (Lessons 9-11) Be sure you can place Malachi on your timeline.

    Is there a king? What is the political setting?

Scriptural Context

2. Read the book then come back and answer the questions.

*3. You'll notice the book is laid out in a series of questions and answers as God dialogues with His people. Be sure you understand what God is saying so you can you can pull out the principles and promises that apply to us today.

Chapter 1

God says	They ask	God Explains	Truths about God
1:2	1:2	1:2-6	

God says	They ask	God explains	Truths about God
1:6	1:6	1:7, 8	1:10, 11, 14

4. Echo/Review. Remember who Edom was from our study of Obadiah? This verse is quoted in Romans 9:6-14. Unless we understand what this means in the context of the whole scripture, we can get a wrong concept of God. Be ready to discuss your findings with the class.

   What is **Malachi 1:2,3** talking about?

*5. Are there any *principles* and/or *promises* from this chapter that apply to us today?

Chapter 2
*Question numbers 6, 7, 8.

God says	They ask:	God Explains	Truths about God
2:2		2:3-12	2:5

God says	They ask	God explains	Truths about God
2:13	2:14	2:14-17	2:16
2:17	2:17	2:17	

9. What else does Scripture have to say about divorce? What do you think the whole picture of divorce is supposed to teach us? Here are two cross-references to get you started. Can you find more?
   Deuteronomy 24:1-4

   Matthew 19:8

   (Which minor prophet talked about marriage?)

*10. Are there any **principles** and/or **promises** from this chapter that apply to us today?

Chapter 3

11. 3:1-3: God is sending them a "Messenger." Notice how that word is a play on Malachi's name. Who does this message/messenger refer to? How does 3:2, 3 fit with everything else?

For fulfillment see: Mt. 11:10, 14

*Question numbers 12, 13.

God says	They ask:	God Explains	Truths about God
3:7, 8	3:7, 8	3:9-12	
3:13	3:13	3:14, 15	

14. How do the people respond in 3:16?

What is God's reaction to their response? 3:17, 18

15. Are there any other *principles* and/or *promises* from this chapter that might apply to us today?

Chapter 4

16. What is the contrast that God gives about the "day that is coming?"

   What was it God wanted them to remember?

Personal Holiness

17. There are many very applicable things in this book. Look back over your answers. Which one stands out to you this week?

If we are going to live by the premise that God's word is true, then we know that "He does not change." The God of Leviticus is the God of the Gospels. He is the God of Acts and the God of the Epistles. He is the God of Revelation.

18. What is the implication of that in your life this week?

19. Meditate on the Memory Verse.
    (Is there a command to obey? Promise to claim? Warning to heed? Something to give thanks for?)

> **Want more on Elijah?**
> *Check out these cross references. You might come up with more questions than you answer!*
>
> *2 Kings 2:11*
>
> *Matthew 11:14*
>
> *Matthew 17:10-13*
>
> *Luke 1:17*
>
> *John 1:21*
>
> *Would you call Jesus coming as a man to die for us a "great and terrible day?" In some ways yes, but in others?? If not, then what is Malachi 4:5 talking about?*

Thoughts.

One of the things I see as we study the Minor Prophets is more emphasis on the heavy handedness of God and less on His love. (Though it is there!) It occurs to me, it is God, dealing with an adolescent nation in the days before grace covered all our sins. The parent of an adolescent is not "the friend." He is the parent. There are bigger lessons during this time to learn about responsibility, consequences and personal integrity. If the parent is constantly covering over those things, the child grows up without an appreciation for the cost of grace. God becomes the one who owes us forgiveness. After all, He let us get into this mess.

So in this last book of the Old Testament, we see God reminding them to "Remember." "Be Holy for I am Holy." Reminding them of their responsibilities as a nation, chosen, set apart for God. Reminding them this is not a game, He is God from the rising of the sun to it's setting, and His name will be praised.

This is our God! Let everything within us Praise His Name!

Truths about God from the Minor Prophets

The Day of the Lord in the Minor Prophets

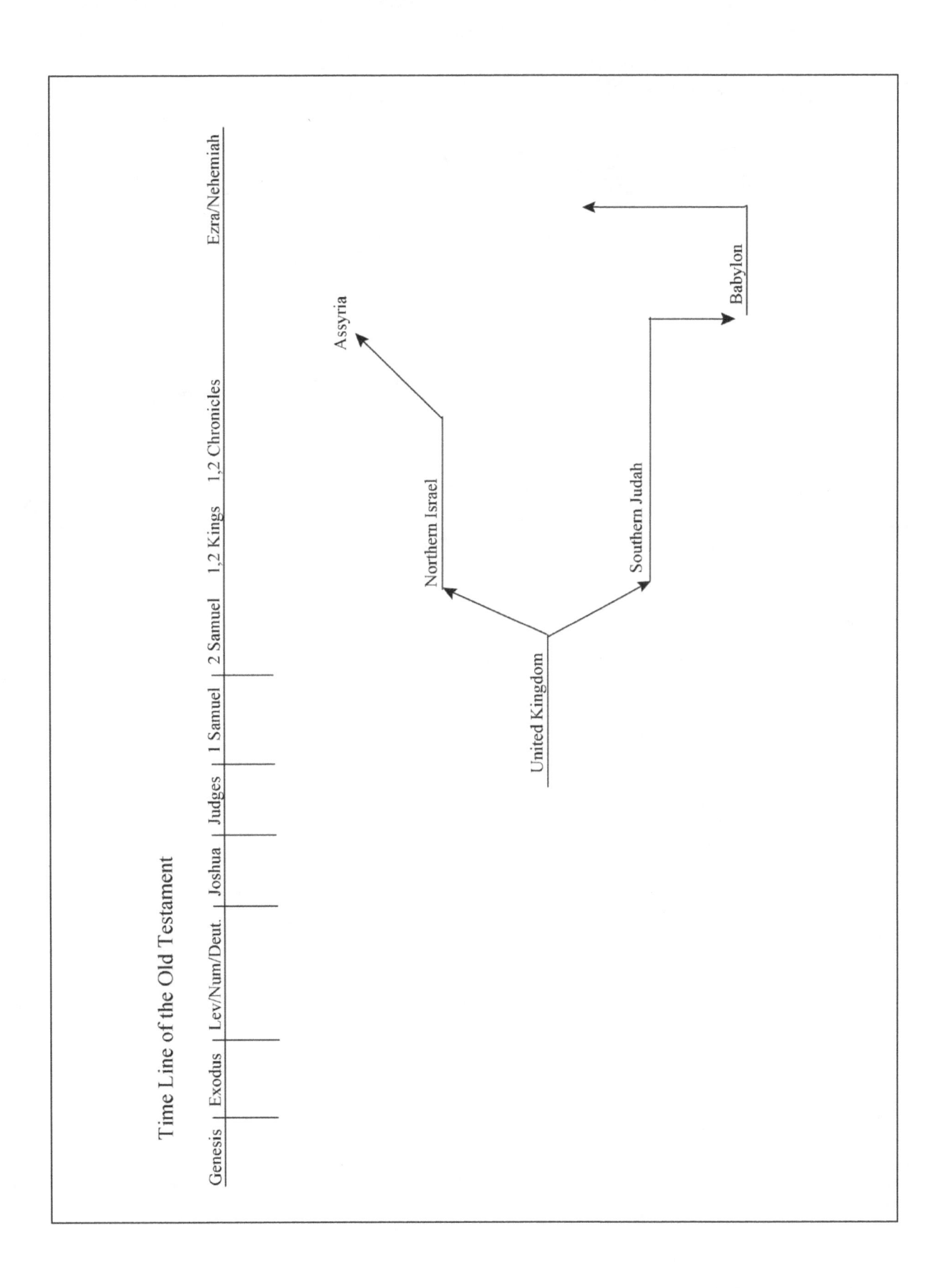

Time Line of the Old Testament

Genesis | Exodus | Lev/Num/Deut. | Joshua | Judges | 1 Samuel | 2 Samuel | 1,2 Kings | 1,2 Chronicles | Ezra/Nehemiah

United Kingdom → Northern Israel → Assyria

United Kingdom → Southern Judah → Babylon →

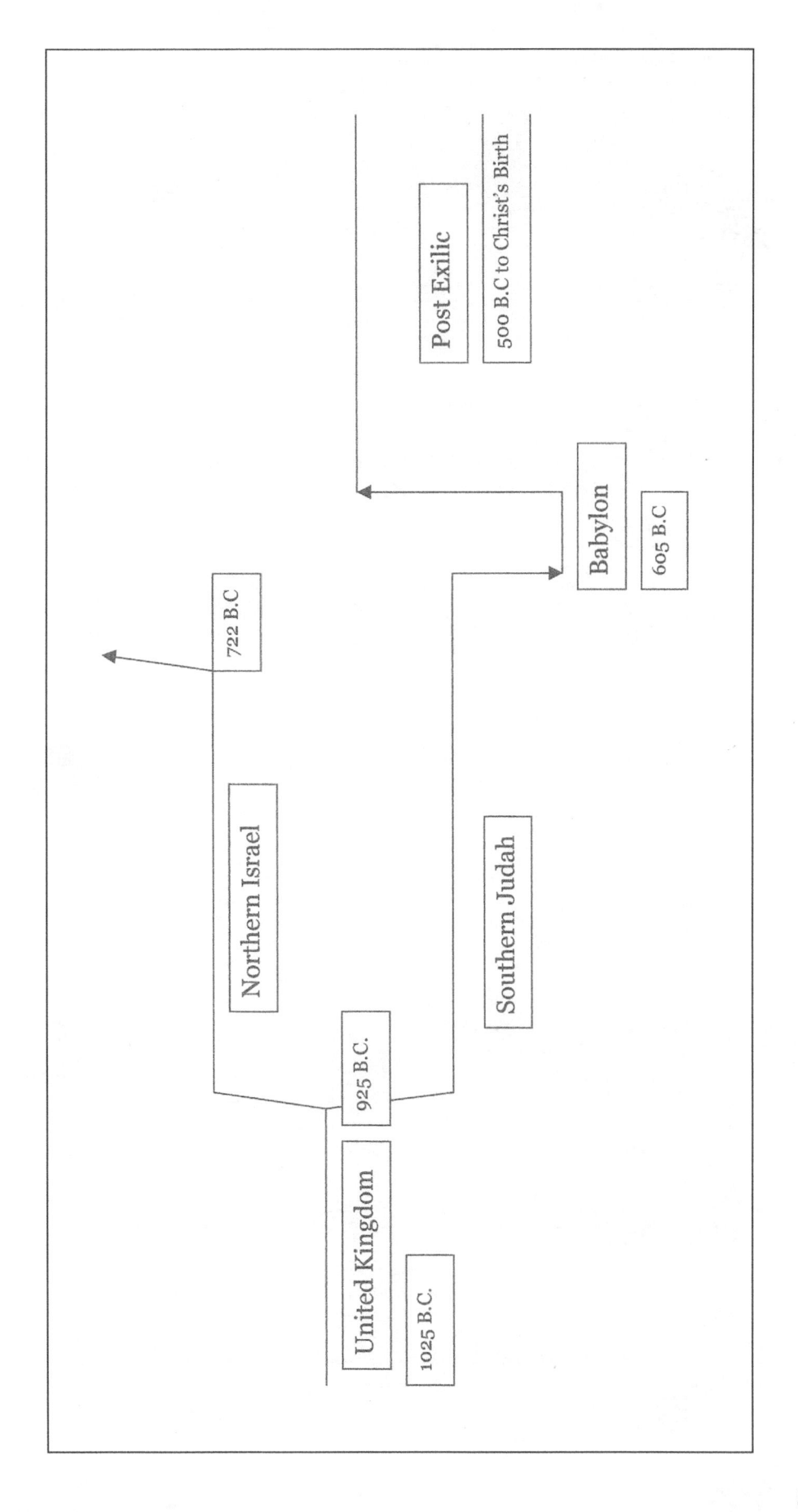

United Kingdom	1025 B.C.
925 B.C.	
Northern Israel	722 B.C
Southern Judah	
Babylon	605 B.C
Post Exilic	500 B.C to Christ's Birth

The Minor Prophets

History of Israel	**Hosea** Mem Verse	**Joel** Mem Verse	**Amos** Mem Verse	**Obadiah/Jonah/Nahum** Mem Verse	**Micah** Mem Verse
	Theme	Theme	Theme	Theme	Theme
	Related Kings	Related Kings	Related Kings	Related Kings	Related Kings
	Memorable Moment	Memorable Moment	Memorable Moment	Memorable Moment	Memorable Moment
Zephaniah Mem Verse	**Habakkuk** Mem Verse	**Haggai** Mem Verse	**Zecharia Part 1** Mem Verse	**Zecharia Part 2** Mem Verse	**Malachi** Mem Verse
Theme	Theme	Theme	Theme	Theme	Theme
Related Kings	Related Kings	Related Kings	Related Kings	Related Kings	Related Kings
Memorable Moment	Memorable Moment	Memorable Moment	Memorable Moment	Memorable Moment	Memorable Moment

Notes

Notes

Made in United States
Cleveland, OH
12 April 2025